TESTIMONIALS

TURN is packed with profoundly simple information to get unstuck and follow your path. As an HR professional, I see people unclear and struggling in their careers; this book will help them thrive. The process transforms what seems impossible, into not only possible, but absolutely tangible. Brilliant read and amazing author. Clara is fun and relatable, which makes TURN not only effective, but enjoyable to read, too!

— Nicole Jones-Gyllstrom, Senior Vice President, Arthur J. Gallagher & Co.

TURN is an inspirational read, and a magnificently simple approach to get congruent with who you are and what you are capable of. Clara's four-step approach to get in touch with what might be getting in the way of your professional progress—and move it out of the way—is powerful! This is a must-read for those wanting to accelerate their careers, pivot to a new career path, or transition back into the work place.

— John Appelgren: Executive Career Coach|Consultant, Lee Hecht Harrison

Engaged employees are better employees. They find purpose in their work, challenge themselves and others, and as a result deliver for their organizations. This attitude and passion is what attracts hiring managers. Clara's guidance is spot on as she challenges us to look deep within, to engage with our various parts and discover where we're meant to contribute our talents. While not an easy journey, it has lifelong implications.

— Katie Weibert: Talent Development Consultant at one of the Big Four Accounting Firms

TURN empowers professionals who want a career change to challenge their inner selves. The four steps are a succinct process to transform fear and get into action. Strongly recommended for anyone who has felt his or her career was held back by misplaced self-doubt.

— Peter McManus: Sales Director, salesforce.com

TURN

4 Steps to Clarity in your Career

TURN

4 Steps to Clarity in your Career

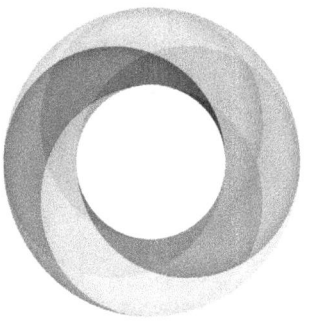

CLARA CHORLEY

Foreword by Arthur Samuel Joseph

Copyright © 2016 by Clara Chorley

All rights reserved.

No portion of this book may be reproduced, stored in a retrieval system, or transmitted in any form or media or by any means, electronic, mechanical, photocopying, recording, or otherwise, without the prior written permission of the author, except in the case of brief quotations embodied in critical articles or reviews.

Your support of the author's right is appreciated.

Cover and interior design by 1106 Design.

TURN
4 Steps to Clarity in Your Career
Chorley, Clara

ISBNs: 978-0-9975961-0-6 (print)
978-0-9975961-1-3 (eBook)

REVISED EDITION
First paperback printing 2013

*To Hal and Sidra Stone for
lovingly introducing me to my parts.*

Contents

Foreword		xi
Introduction		xv
Chapter One	Parts	1
Chapter Two	Incongruency	17
Chapter Three	The Human Challenge	37
Chapter Four	The TURN Process *Step One:* Transform	49
Chapter Five	The TURN Process *Step Two:* Unwind	75
Chapter Six	The TURN Process *Step Three:* Resolve	87
Chapter Seven	The TURN Process *Step Four:* Next	105
Chapter Eight	Rwanda	131
About the Author		143

Foreword

The single greatest deterrent to living life on our terms is that there is no one to tell us what to do. In *TURN: 4 Steps to Clarity in Your Career*, Clara teaches you "how to tell yourself what to do" and, in this way, respectfully helps you empower yourself. She is a "pragmatic visionary," for, as you will read in this powerful book, she has not only assisted many others in gaining rewarding professional lives, but she has also taken action and turned her own dreams into a vision fulfilled. Clara lives what she teaches, and, in my experience, that is rare.

Clarity is the first step in having the career you want. Everybody has dreams, but all the dreamer does is dream them. In this wonderful book, Clara will show you how to turn your dreams into a vision fulfilled. You will know what you want, and you will appreciate yourself in a deeper, kinder, more satisfying way by the time you complete this book. After all, it is not merely what we *do* that matters—it is equally *who we are.* In the current professional climate, this has never been so true.

I have known Clara for a number of years. She embodies courage and wisdom, and lives in what I refer to as Deeper Listening. She knows how to tune into her body's broadcast system, tune out the "white noise" of other people's opinions and ideas, and follow her own inner compass. In my experience, this is the only sustainable way to live a fulfilling life, and this book gives you access to transformational tools so that you can do the same.

It is an honor and privilege for me to know Clara and to write a foreword for the second edition of this truly important book. It is not merely a game-changer—it is a life-changer. Clara is your due north, and this edition focuses directly on navigating through career change while providing tools and insights that also positively impact all areas of your life.

As the final quote in this book, by Nelson Mandela, states: "It always seems impossible until it's done." Nothing truly is impossible, but it can seem that way. In this brilliant book, Clara provides a step-by-step map for clarifying your journey and shows you that what you want is absolutely possible.

I know you will enjoy and be transformed by the discoveries that await you.

—Arthur Samuel Joseph
Author of *Voice of a Leader* and *Vocal Power*

Clients include Ernst and Young, Deloitte and Touche, the Ritz-Carlton Hotel Company, the NFL Network, and ESPN.
www.vocalawareness.com

Introduction

Intelligent women and men tell me every day how there's something they want but could never have, or someone they want to stand up to but are too afraid, or how nothing works out for them no matter how hard they try.

While we move through life often believing that external factors are standing in our way, it's my experience that it's actually internal factors that block us the most. I find it a relief to know that what's in my way isn't the government, my partner, friends, children, my financial situation, or where I live. Instead, what's in the way is how I am thinking about my life, the choices I'm making, and what my relationship with risk, fear, and, perhaps most importantly, myself, is like.

Often, people know deep inside that what they're doing isn't what they really want to do, or they can't seem to find a job doing what they want to do. That's what TURN is for. To assist you in being your best self and to help you find the work that best fits you, so that you can make the difference with your life that you are here to make.

The job game has changed, competition is higher than ever, and, with the Internet, the application process has become even more impersonal. Our ability to be our best selves, to shine in the world, and let our strengths lead is more important than ever. We can no longer afford to tuck away our insecurities and hide from what and who we're designed to do and be in the world. There's too much competition. To stand out, whether it's in person or on a piece of paper, you have to be yourself and own what you're good at.

TURN is a simple, easy-on-the-emotions methodology that helps people identify what blocks their progress, unblock it, and move forward. This directly translates to career clarity and success.

The original edition of TURN came out in 2013. I became inspired to revise that edition as TURN evolved, as the job market evolved, and as my experience of how this process was impacting my clients shifted and deepened. Additionally, as my audiences have become more focused on career change and job seeking, it made sense to include examples and content from the professional side of life.

Whether you're transitioning into a completely new career, wanting to change the organization you work for, or trying to figure out how to go to the next level with your skill set, TURN can assist you as it has many others over the years. As experiential learning increases the likelihood of lasting change, I've made this a workbook. Grab a pen, participate fully in the exercises, mark up this book, and then take what you learn and go find your best-fit work.

Chapter One

Parts

If you took out the excessive drinking and smoking, my life looked pretty good. I grew up in Birmingham, England, and went to an all-girls school with green uniforms, skirts that couldn't be too short, ties that couldn't be too skinny, and socks that I was constantly told to pull up (literally—I preferred the scruffy look, and that didn't go down well). I learned math, physics, geography, piano, ballet, grass hockey, and more. It was a wonderful and diverse education, and by the time I turned fifteen, the only place I wanted to be was the local pub.

I was happy hanging out there, smoking and drinking illegally with my closest friends. Maybe we went to school first, but not always. We went to the pub much too young, and we stayed there much too long.

I had friends, a great school, decent social skills, and knew a few cute boys. My chances at a successful life were looking good! When school ended at eighteen years old, I moved into my own apartment and began a secretarial certificate. Once I sort of knew how to type, I quit the program, and I was surprised to be hired as a junior secretary, in an advertising agency, shortly after. I was just about the only girl in my year who hadn't gone to university, and I was a terrible secretary.

Looking back, none of the job options I learned about from the career counselors at school fit me. I chose secretary because I was told it'd be a "good job to fall back on," and at that time, I could think of no other options. So I went with someone else's idea and told myself I was "buying some time."

That advertising job became the first of many that I fell back on and walked away from. "Walked away" because I believed I was destined for more. I furiously pursued my calling, my purpose—otherwise known as *The Search for Something I'm Really Good At That Makes a Difference and Feels Like Me.* Three years and three jobs later, still searching, I moved to London to reluctantly attend university in an attempt to join the masses and delete the belief that I wasn't smart enough. One year into the environmental policy degree, I surprised everyone, including myself, and emigrated to America. Another incomplete educational endeavor, but I did delete the "I'm not smart" belief.

I dressed well, spoke well, was fairly pretty, dated boys, drank like a fish, and smoked like a chimney. I was a seemingly normal, healthy Brit. I even won a car! Right before going to university in London, I worked for an insurance company, and one of the managers challenged me to sign up five new policies in a week. If I did, he said, he would give me a car. So I worked my tail off and signed up six. It took a while to get the car, but I got it, and that Mini Metro moved me to London shortly thereafter. I was good at what I invested my mind and energy into.

But no one really knew what was going on inside me.

As the years passed, I tried a number of different jobs in different industries and travelled extensively. But under the surface, there was a deep sense that something was missing and that something wasn't quite right. I didn't fit, and I felt deeply dissatisfied, unhappy, and unsettled. No matter how far I travelled or how many successes I racked up, this feeling stayed with me. I tried career counselors, personality tests, therapists, and volunteering all over the world.

And nothing seemed to work. I suppose the jobs did get more interesting over time, but I *knew* that I wasn't in my sweet spot. Something continued to feel incongruent on a couple of levels: the work I was doing and the way I felt about myself.

Deep down, I knew that unless I fundamentally changed how I saw and felt about myself, I would not be able to clarify the work that belonged to me. I had to become the woman who did the work I imagined. And at that time, I imagined getting paid to travel, speak, and listen to people ("listening" was my version of "coaching" before I knew what coaching was). But my self-image was of a broken, fearful, reactive young girl. Not congruent. Not only did I have no idea how to change things, but I was pretty afraid that they weren't changeable.

It wasn't until I discovered parts that I got unstuck.

Introducing Parts

I share my story because it's not unique. It's easy to relate to. Women and men all over the world have walked in these same shoes—trying to figure out how to feel congruent with who they are and what they do. It can seem elusive, but people are doing it, so we know it's possible.

None of us can get to where we want to go by ourselves. We can't see our nose without a mirror, and it's the same with our inner world. We are made up of wounded, playful, brave, ashamed, terrified, loving, aggressive, intelligent parts. Some of them we're aware of, and some of them direct from behind the scenes. Until we know the parts who talk us out of the job we want, stop us from drawing boundaries with co-workers, or frighten us away from experiences we know we want to have, we are at their mercy.

And *that* is at the core of what it means to be stuck.

On my own journey I have hired coaches, therapists, energy workers, spiritual advisors, and body workers. I discovered the different parts that kept me running around the planet, quitting pretty great jobs, reaching for the bottle of wine, avoiding intimacy, and feeling like a huge failure.

As I found and engaged with these parts, my self-esteem, confidence, and awareness around what I deeply wanted and needed began to change. I finally started to feel like *me*—and listen to and care for myself in a much kinder, more loving way. I discovered my intuition and my inner Wise Woman. I found and fundamentally changed my relationship with the part of me that believed she deserved to suffer, and I found some peace. I started to feel like I had some control over my life, like I was finally in the driver's seat. I stopped using alcohol, and my career morphed into something that fit and felt like me.

I had to re-learn that not only was it *safe* to feel joy and aliveness but that those feelings were actually magnetic—I needed them to *attract* the work and life I wanted.

It's the same for you.

Different Parts

We're complex humans, made up of a fascinating, unique mix of different parts. Think for a moment about who you are and how you behave when you're with your boss, versus with your boy/girl friend, versus a complete stranger at the bus stop. Think about how sometimes you feel and think angry thoughts and how, at other times, you're joyful and grateful, and at other times, you're judging like you're in a competition to win the Most Judgmental Human award.

These different personalities are all different parts of you. And each part has its own opinions, motivations, and intelligence. Some universal parts are:

The Pusher—the part that is go-go-go and has you constantly doing things

The Inner Critic—the part that finds something wrong with absolutely everything you say and do

The Pleaser—the part that is committed to pleasing absolutely *everyone,* probably before pleasing you.

Some parts are more likely to express on our bad days than on the days when we feel good.

Here's an example:

David gets turned down for another job. Once again, he is rejected after the second round of interviews.

Today, David isn't feeling his best. On arriving home, he paces the room and vents to his girlfriend, Jane, about how wrong those people are, how biased they are, how pointless it all is, and how they should move to another state or even another country. David feels anger. His angry part has a point of view and expresses it clearly.

Conversely, today David is feeling optimistic and confident. He's calm. On arriving home, his supportive part comes out with Jane. He sits down next to her and chats about how, even though he's disappointed, he believes that it was right that he didn't get the job; he knows he's on track and that all will be well. He might even give her a big hug and smile.

The Role of Parts

Different parts express at different times, and different parts are committed to different outcomes. Some block us from having what we want professionally. For example:

1. A fearful part might stop us from getting clear about the work we want to do because something about it feels too threatening.
2. A confused part might cause us to doubt what we know is true about what we want and what we're capable of.
3. An angry part might sabotage our efforts to move forward by getting us into fights, activating momentary amnesia, causing accidents, or saying the wrong things at the wrong times ("What was I thinking?!" moments).

Until we become aware of the parts of our inner world that are more committed to things not changing, and until we learn why they're doing what they're doing, we remain at their mercy, watching our lives go through the same patterns again and again, and feeling powerless to stop the cycle.

STORY A

Tara knew that there was work out there for her that she'd enjoy and be good at, but she couldn't figure out what it was. She knew that discovering what it was played a vital role in her feeling fulfilled and that her life had meaning. She knew a few of the things she was good at, but mostly she knew what she didn't want, and couldn't seem to get clear.

STORY B

Andrew knew exactly what he wanted to do: he wanted to be a brand designer for start-up organizations. Currently he was a computer programmer who designed very occasionally on the side. He didn't know how to transition from one to the other, and he worried about financial security. But, like Tara, he knew that figuring this out was vital if he was to feel good about who he was and what he was doing with his life. He was stuck.

Both Tara and Andrew started working the steps of TURN. They began to see how different parts were playing important roles in their careers. As a result:

STORY A

Tara discovered that there were parts of her who were scared of getting clear about her career because they feared she'd lose the love and approval of her family if she became professionally successful. Every time she was on the verge of a breakthrough of some sort or a change of job, she'd suddenly experience either inexplicable fear or strong "rational" reasons for not making that change.

STORY B

Andrew discovered that part of him was afraid of losing financial security, and he needed to take some practical steps before moving forward. The part of him who needed financial security wanted a certain amount of savings in the bank, to pay off two of his credit card debts, and for him to only eat out three nights a week—not the seven he was currently enjoying. And until he did those things, that part would give him a litany of scary reasons why making the leap would end in catastrophe, essentially blocking his ability to think creatively, and stopping him in his tracks.

If a strong enough part of you is not onboard with you making changes, you simply won't be able to. It's like trying to reason with a toddler who's throwing a fit. And most of us know that that just doesn't work.

Kindness

It's easy to dislike certain parts of ourselves, especially when we think their main job is to hold us back from what we want. But not liking certain things we do, say, or think can lead to some pretty unkind internal conversations, *"I can't believe I just did that!" "I'm such an idiot!" "Only I would make a mistake like that!"* Let me say right here that if you genuinely want your life to change, being hard on yourself is not the way to go.

Consider this . . .

Tom shows up 45 minutes late without calling. You've waited around, he's been late before, and you're mad. You run conversations through your mind, and plan on telling him exactly what you think if he ever arrives. How thoughtless! He didn't even call!

And Tom's side of things . . . Tom is doing his best to arrive on time. Unfortunately, fixing an unexpected flat tire steals his time, and, by the time he reaches for his phone to call, the battery is dead. He knows that being on time is important to you, and he eventually shows up, feeling guilty and nervous about your response.

In the absence of knowing what happened to Tom, it's easy to leap to judgment. Hopefully, though, as you read his side of things, you found compassion and forgiveness. This dynamic is going on inside many of us every day, especially with parts that have been with us for a long time. For example: how natural it feels to criticize ourselves when we do something wrong or imperfectly (we'll take a deeper dive into the Inner Critic in Chapter Four). We leap to judgment over our own behaviors before we pause, assume best intentions, and take the time to understand what happened.

Understanding why we do what we do not only transforms unconscious behaviors into conscious choices but also leads us to feel more understood and accepted by—guess who? By *ourselves!* This is at the core of self-esteem and self-love—indispensable traits if you're navigating a career transition.

When it comes to the people in our lives we, for the most part, get to choose who we spend time with. When it comes to different parts of us, we don't get to walk away. The good news is that the parts that are hardest to love usually hold the juiciest wisdom and can have a dramatically positive influence on our progress in life once we start to understand and care about them.

Kindness is a gift we can give to ourselves and to those we love. We all make mistakes; that's not going to change. Tom may be consistently late, but maybe he's an insightful listener. Over time, you can adjust the relationship with Tom so that you're not waiting around for him, but you get to keep the insightful listening. Relying on Tom to be on time will, guaranteed, lead to ongoing frustration and hurt your relationship. In a similar way, relying on a highly critical part of yourself as the only one with which to assess another person or situation means you'll certainly miss out on well-rounded and balanced viewpoints, as well as relationships and opportunities.

Turning In

To have careers and lives that fulfill us, we must turn inward and face our selves. Through TURN, you will begin to learn more about your selves. You'll discover that the feeling of not being good enough belongs to part of you but that there's also a part that is well aware of your value. You'll discover parts that have the key to the career you want. You'll discover parts that are excited and ready to go, as well as parts with their feet firmly on the brake. You'll learn how to transform the parts that feel like obstacles to what you want, and you'll gain important tools for slowing down and accessing the wisest part of you, your intuition. In addition to that, you'll finish up TURN with a personalized strategic plan to move you forward.

More is in your control than you currently realize.

IMPORTANT NOTE: I'm focusing a great deal of these initial chapters on inviting you to clarify who you are and what you're facing in your career in terms of parts. There are parts of you that hold core beliefs, parts that belong to you and ones that don't, parts designed to help you to fit in, and opposite parts that are creating conflict and "stuckness." Moving into the

TURN process with this foundational information will make following the steps faster and easier.

Next let's look at what happens when key parts are out of balance and seem to get lost.

Chapter Two

Incongruency

Try this on: Start to think about beliefs as belonging to parts of you. Instead of saying, *"I believe in unicorns,"* you might now say, *"Part of me believes in unicorns, and another part thinks I'm nuts to believe in unicorns."* There might be a part of you we'll call *Fear* that believes you'll never have the career you want, but there is also a part we'll call *Certainty* that believes as long as you stick at it, it's just a matter of time. Or perhaps *Certainty* has been beaten into submission by *Fear*. This can happen. Sometimes stronger parts dominate. And when this happens, you can find yourself stuck in an ongoing power struggle with *Fear*. This is incongruent, and it's a showstopper when we want something to change in our lives.

Definition

I n c o n g r u e n t :
not matching or in agreement with
something; not suitable or not fitting well
with something else:

*Violence is incongruent with our values
and legal system.*

The good news is that, while you may be primarily aware of only *Fear*, *Certainty* does exist inside you—it's simply temporarily lost. *Fear* is not *all* of you, the *entirety* of your being, your personality, your makeup. It's just become a dominant part that is taking up a lot of room, which leaves you stuck and feeling off balance.

Fitting In

Beliefs thrive in our communities. Commonly held points-of-view that keep things organized and functioning often integrate into our own psyches as we're growing up. Parts form inside us and attempt to merge these external norms into who we are so that we fit in and belong.

Clearly it doesn't always work out that way.

Here in the United States of America, there's a widespread belief that it's possible to have a successful business just because we're good at something: "I'm good at this thing, so I'm going to start a business." And then we make a million dollars.

Not in England, when I was growing up.

Back then, unqualified entrepreneurship was not looked on favorably. Don't even think about starting a business unless you have a Master's or a PhD. It was even difficult to get a decent-paying job without higher education. This resulted in my growing up with a strong part that convinced me that I had to follow a very strict, pre-determined path in order to fit in and be successful: first high school, then university, graduate school, job, marriage, promotion, children, another promotion, retirement, have fun, die. And whenever I wasn't following this path, I felt like I was failing.

My internal dialogue sounded something like this:

> *"I've got to pass all my exams and get a degree and probably a Master's, too, if I'm ever going to be professionally successful. I should know what I want to do when I leave school at eighteen so that I can go straight to university.*

I'm meant to get married and have two children and a cat—which terrifies me, because I can barely take care of myself. And then I'm going to work hard in this career that I've always known that I wanted. But I don't know what it is. How do people find that out? Doesn't it matter whether I like it or want to do it? What if I'm no good at what I want to do?! And then I'm going to retire, if I make it that far, and then, maybe, I'll finally start traveling and enjoying my life. And this sounds awful to me but everyone else gets it and is doing well. I'm the only one who isn't. There must be something wrong with me!"

Argggh!

This is what happens internally when the beliefs we inhale from our environment conflict with who we are at our core. Again, there's incongruency.

I knew that that wasn't my true path at all.

What about flip from job to job, work in an Indian slum, move to a different continent, and not marry at 25? Why was no one promoting that life path? The challenge, however, was that part of me had internalized the belief that, if I didn't take the higher-education route, I would never have a successful career, let alone a happy life. I honestly struggled with that for years. I'd start taking steps toward a life that fit me better, and then this invisible rubber band would pull me back to what I'd learned as a child. It wasn't until I found the courage to follow beliefs that were truly *mine* that the trajectory of my career and life started to change.

YOUR TURN

Take a minute and think of some of your own beliefs and expectations about work and career—from the past as well as some that you're facing now as you move through this transition. Consider the ones that conflict with the core of who you are.

How do you know if a belief is a core one? It might inspire and energize you, feel exciting and risky, or it could feel easy and almost neutral. It just belongs, and, deep down, you know it.

Perhaps you're comfortable with some beliefs, such as, *"It's important to work hard,"* and perhaps you struggle with others, such as, *"Getting paid well and doing what I love aren't compatible,"* or *"Great jobs with great co-workers don't exist."*

As you write, watch for opposites such as, *"I have to work hard to earn decent money,"* followed by,

"No, I don't! I just haven't figured out how to do it differently yet."

When it comes to work and career, some of my beliefs are:

_____

_____

_____

_____

_____

_____

_____

_____

_____

Put a star next to the ones you think might truly belong to you—the ones that feel like they resonate with your core. Whether they "make sense" to your "rational" mind or not, put a star by them. Hint: they'll feel good to you. You will recognize them because, when you say them out loud, you feel ease, resonance, and even joy.

We believe what we believe for good reason. When we over-ride beliefs that are uniquely ours, it's usually for very good reason.

Meet John . . .

John's Story

John is a self-proclaimed couch potato. He didn't used to be. But as the months of unemployment passed by, he found his motivation gradually decreasing. A year later, he could barely get up from the couch.

The combination of not working, failed interviews, dead-end networking, and unacknowledged applications resulted in the, "I give up" part of John taking over. He wasn't that clear even before he got laid off, and finding clarity is harder when the security of a paycheck is gone. The voices and beliefs of different parts had worn him out, "I want this!" "No, I should be going for that." "But wait, I should really be going for this other thing." "Oh, I give up." Part of John knows what to do to get out of this stuck place, because he's smart and has plenty of experience. But other parts are more committed to eating chips on the couch. He wants to be in action but just can't seem to get going.

John had a dream of being in a management position with a company that was effecting positive change. He knew what steps to take to get there, but fear kept him from taking them. An invisible energy kept pulling him back to a status quo and a couch that was familiar and comforting. Perhaps you have your own version of the couch—the fridge, Internet, smartphone, being busy, being frozen by perfectionism, doing the wrong job. John was smart, but when I met him, he felt like he was on a roller coaster. "Do I want this, or do I want that?" "I can do it!" "No! I can't." "I would be a great manager!" "No, I'd be terrible!"

Different parts of John couldn't come to agreement, and what was clear was that John certainly was not in the driver's seat of his own career. He hired me to help him get unstuck, clear, and back into action. As we coached, he began to identify parts that were stopping him. Two were particularly significant. The first part told him, *"Just get a job. You can't get paid well **and** do work you love."* The other part said, *"You're not smart enough to do what you really want to do, so don't bother trying."* Neither was motivating.

Why we do what we do

It's very difficult to access the parts of us that are inspired to go after what we want when they're over-ridden by parts that believe we're not smart enough, or we can't make decent money doing what we want, or we're a failure and should quit every time something doesn't go our way. Heading to the proverbial couch can seem like a better option when parts like this are running the show.

I sat with John, and we talked about what he wanted. He was trying to get a clear picture of it in his mind. As I invited him deeper into the conversation, he opened up and shared a story from when he was a little boy.

His primary caregiver was his grandmother, and she used to help him with his math homework. She'd pull out flash cards, on which were numbers and problems. This was her way of teaching him. Picture Grandma on one side of the kitchen table and young John on the other. She would show him cards with problems such as $2 + 2 = ?$ on them, and he would have to say the answers. Addition, subtraction, multiplication, and division—nothing was excluded.

His grandmother was very generous to take all that time to work with him. And at the same time, she was impatient and became annoyed when he sometimes couldn't understand that $2 + 2 = 4$. *"What do you mean, it's three?!" "What do you mean, it's five?!"* Through these experiences, a part of John was formed that decided *It's not safe to make mistakes.*

As a result of this, John learned to compensate. Over the years, he would get jobs that he enjoyed and wanted, but part of him wasn't comfortable making mistakes. This impacted his learning, strained his relationships at work, and meant he had his guard up most of the time. He constantly felt that, on some level, he would mess everything up. Instead of asking for help, he'd try to figure things out on his own and offer up only work he felt was absolutely correct. This often resulted in missed deadlines and frustrated co-workers because, even with this level of vigilance, he still made mistakes.

In a position that mattered most to him, John couldn't get himself to reveal some fatal errors he was aware of. Had he done so, he would have positively changed the direction of a large project. But, instead of sharing these mistakes with his boss, he worked frantically behind the scenes trying to fix them. He was terrified of being reprimanded or even fired. Ultimately, the project failed, and John was fired.

As he and I uncovered this story, he started to piece together how experiences like this led right back to what had happened with his grandmother.

John identified a protective part that was working diligently to make sure that he was never seen to make a mistake—especially if an authority figure was involved. The love, attention, and approval of his grandmother had been absolutely vital to John when he was young, and the job of this protective part was to make sure that his little boy never again felt the pain of losing this love. Unfortunately, the protective part did this by hiding mistakes, which was a strategy that made sense at the time—but not for John as a grown man.

As John dialogued with this protective part (you'll learn dialoguing in Chapter Four), he noticed that it started to relax its grip, became aware that the strategy it was using of hiding mistakes wasn't working, and opened up to doing things differently. In turn, John became less afraid of making mistakes. As his energy and motivation returned, the grown man inside him started to lead the way.

Tracking back to the recent or distant past can be a powerful tool that reveals out-of-date beliefs we might have about ourselves. We discover that we're not lazy, we're not a waste of time, and we're not unclear. By identifying the part of himself that had been working so hard to protect a little boy who had been afraid of losing Grandma's love, John became more able to handle his mistakes. He started to take some steps toward the management job he wanted.

The need to belong and be accepted can run very deep. Parts form when we're young in response to the people around us, because their presence in our lives often fulfills deep, basic human needs. Primary caregivers, regardless of how challenging they might be, are often a source of belonging, safety, familiarity, and home.

YOUR TURN

As you look back at your relationships with primary caregivers or people in authority when you were young, what beliefs do you notice you might have formed in order to fit in with your family, community, or workplace? Take a moment and write some notes here.

Some examples.

I believe that:
... playing, dancing, and singing are a natural part of self-expression.

... I'm really smart.

... sadness shows weakness, and anger shows strength.

... I don't have a right to say, "No."

... it's safe and fun to explore the world!

Some of my beliefs:

_____

_____

_____

_____

_____

_____

_____

_____

_____

_____

_____

_____

_____

Put a star next to three of the beliefs that you've just identified. Choose big ones—ones that feel most familiar or resonant to you. Now write them as belonging to a part. For example: Part of me believes that the job market is too competitive in my area.

1. Part of me believes _____

   _____

2. Part of me believes _____

   _____

3. Part of me believes _____

   _____

Notice how you feel, when you write it that way.

Next, write the opposite of what these beliefs would be (go ahead and do this whether you're in touch with this opposite or not). For example: An opposite part of me believes that I have more options than I'm aware of currently.

1. An opposite part of me believes _____

   _____

2. An opposite part of me believes _____

   _____

3. An opposite part of me believes _____

   _____

Once you complete this list, I invite you to notice any new awarenesses. Some questions to ponder . . . When you wrote down the opposite beliefs, which ones felt more like you? What is different about how you feel when you write a belief that belongs to you, versus one that is taken on from someone or somewhere else? Maybe you don't know who or where it came from—it just doesn't feel good anymore. What comes up when you imagine reclaiming a part that belongs to you?

Take a few minutes and capture your awarenesses here:

Incongruency | 33

The good news is that, while we all have many parts inside of us, there are a limited number of Primary Parts that carry the big-kahuna beliefs that are running us. If these particular beliefs don't align with us at our core, we'll be stopped in life. My guess is that you might have a conflict going on with a part or two of you, and that's why you feel stuck or unclear.

You Being You

Many of us find ourselves either doing work that was suggested to us at a young age, doing something our mother or father did, doing something we happen to be good at, or doing what we don't want to do. When this is the case, it usually means that, somewhere along the line, we disowned core parts that would naturally lead us to our best-fit work and lives, in exchange for Primary Parts that were more committed to protecting us and keeping us safe.

Recall a time when you felt really *you*. Remember how things just seemed to flow? There was probably a sense of well-being and ease about life, and you felt good about yourself—as if you were connected to yourself in a full, complete way and perhaps to something bigger than you that was on your side. People and opportunities seemed to arrive right when you needed them, what you asked for showed up, and you probably felt joyful.

This is what I call fulfillment. Fulfillment is the feeling generated when we are aligned internally, which means our decisions are being driven by beliefs that truly belong to us—not something we were told, not something we decided based on a painful experience.

The goal of TURN is to return you to this natural state.

Next we're going to dive into Primary Parts so that you can learn what they are and where they might be showing up in your professional life. Then you'll be ready for the TURN process.

Chapter Three

The Human Challenge

We often do not question the things we think. We rarely slow down for long enough to understand the pulls and pushes of conflicting motivations that run us—let alone become aware of the dominant ones, the ones we're most familiar with and how they're running us. Each time we start to move forward, something deep inside seems to stop us.

As I've mentioned before, beliefs belong to parts of us, and there are many parts. However, some play bigger roles than others—they're the CEOs of your life and are known as Primary Parts. If one of your Primary Parts rules with the belief that you don't deserve to have money, love, *and* work that fulfills you, then that will run your life until you find and embrace the part that knows you *do* deserve to have it all. For John, the part that was protecting him from losing love and connection was inadvertently stopping him from excelling at work he loved. This was a Primary Part for John, and those parts are usually formed when we're young. Their main job is to protect us and make sure we survive.

For John to go for the work he really wanted, it meant he had to be comfortable with authority, speaking his truth, sharing uncomfortable news, managing people. But the part of him that associated all authority figures with that experience with his grandmother prevented the adult John from taking necessary risks in order to learn how to be a great manager. This Primary Part was still protecting the little boy in him from pain and was unwilling to relinquish this role. And because John didn't pause to explore what part(s) might be controlling his choices, he just continued to live with a deep dissatisfaction until he couldn't anymore, mainly because he was out of work and out of money.

Have you noticed that this is often what it takes? A wake-up call. And the longer we put something off, the louder the alarm.

Up until John's wake-up call, he did what many of us do—because the part of him committed to his emotional safety was a Primary Part, it felt "normal" to him, so, rather than question it, he struggled and fought with it. John was fired from a job he loved for not being transparent about mistakes, and those mistakes cost the company dearly. But his other option would have been to reveal the mistakes, and that felt terrifying to his younger parts. So, for him, it was an unconscious catch-22 that eventually sent him to the couch.

However, John did have an alternative, and he chose it a couple of years later, after the wake-up call. He took the opportunity to look into the mirror and question whether the negative way he felt about himself was even true and how his own actions had led to the outcome of losing his job. This woke him up to a pattern in him almost as old as he was, and that was the start of his freedom.

YOUR TURN

Start to consider some earlier beliefs you took on and where you might have reinforced them over the years. Feel free to include career and personal stories.

Part of me believes:	Experiences that have reinforced this:
1. It's more important to get paid well than love my work.	1. My last three jobs have paid me well, and I can't stand them!
2. I'm not smart enough to have the job I want.	2. I keep doing jobs that I could do in my sleep. I'm bored!

Part of me believes:	Experiences that have reinforced this:

Part of me believes:	Experiences that have reinforced this:

How Parts Affect Us

Different parts affect how we think, feel, and behave. By now you're perhaps aware of a new part or two that's influencing your life in either positive or negative ways. But it's when things happen in life that we get to really see who the main players are inside of us, simply by noticing how we react.

For example: A co-worker gets a pay raise, and I don't. Well, if I have a Primary Part that believes that life is generous and fair, I'll probably respond with, *"I'm happy for that co-worker—they earned it; I wonder if there's something I can do to get one."* Conversely, if I have a Primary Part that believes I never get rewarded and life's just not fair, I might respond with, *"Why didn't I get a raise? This company doesn't value me at all, and that co-worker never deserved it. This is the last time I work this hard!"*

I'm not saying that there aren't times when people aren't valued by the organization they work for. I am pointing to how they respond when faced with a scenario like this.

When the recession hit, if I was laid off and have a Primary Part that believes that bad things always happen to me, I might have responded with *"I will never be hired, and I will probably lose my home."* That would probably send me to the couch pretty quickly. But if I'm run by a Primary Part that believes that things work out and that this is an opportunity to find something better, I might have responded with *"This is difficult, but I know I have what it takes. What resources do I have around me? I'm ready for a better fit!"*

Our responses have a direct impact on how we feel about our situation and ourselves, and, subsequently, they then impact the actions we take.

Changing Parts

As you discover parts of you that are stopping you from moving forward, it wouldn't be surprising if you started to wonder how you might change or even get rid of some of them! So, let me lead with this: No one likes to be changed—not your friend, your partner, your co-worker, your boss, and certainly not you. The same goes for your parts.

Typically, when we want someone to change something about themselves, we directly or indirectly let them know that we don't like that thing they do, and, therefore, we want them to change it. And that rarely feels good—to either party.

> *Susan wants her boss, Lisa, to ask her how she is when they first meet in the morning, rather than dive straight into work tasks. Every time Lisa arrives and starts to talk about work, Susan gets tense, withdraws, and stops smiling, and a judgmental voice starts to go off in her head about how Lisa doesn't care about her and overworks her. Lisa feels Susan's withdrawal, but it's in the back of her mind, so she doesn't mention it. However, Lisa finds herself feeling uncomfortable and unconsciously pulling back because she doesn't feel good around Susan. She focuses more on getting quickly through the task list.*

We feel it when people don't accept parts of us, and most of us want to be loved and accepted for all of who we are—our strengths, our weakness, our good sides, and our mess. Have you ever sat with someone you felt completely comfortable with? Someone you could be completely yourself with? A therapist? A boss or mentor? A lover? A friend? I hope so, because, if you have, you know that this feeling can exist only in the absence of being judged. When you're with someone who doesn't need you to change, there's this strange thing that occurs. We want to change! We want to be our best so that they continue to hold us in that light. When we make a mistake and we're given feedback but not judged, we improve, we learn.

Susan wants to know her boss, Lisa, better, partly because Susan is a people-person and partly because she finds Lisa's directness and productivity a little daunting. Susan struggles with being direct and knows this about herself. She also knows it would be a helpful skill to develop. The next morning, when Lisa arrives, Susan smiles broadly, and, with a deep breath and pounding heart, she initiates the morning conversation with, "At some point, I'd love to hear how your weekend was."

Lisa knows she's more task oriented than relationship oriented and secretly would really like to cultivate some of Susan's people skills, but she feels awkward. When Susan shows a genuine desire to know her more (rather than disapproval of who she was being), Lisa feels accepted, and this is followed by a willingness to share some personal information . . . after they get through the tasks at hand!

To change any part of yourself, you must first accept it without judgment. Sorry, but that's just the way it goes. Your parts are no different from anyone else's, and no one likes to be judged. In order to accept parts you most dislike, judge, or struggle with, there is a powerful assumption I'm going to invite you to take on:

Every Part Has a Positive Intention

The driving motivation behind the behaviors, thoughts, and feelings of every single part of you is positive. Even parts that seem to be stopping you or berating you or ruining your love life, even the ugly, dark parts all have a positive intention, usually one of protection.

Karen had a part that when she got home at the end of day, she couldn't stop from berating her husband. She'd find everything wrong that she possibly could and mention it. Through the TURN process, she learned that the berating part was protecting her from giving more. Karen spent her days in a job that took everything she had. She fake-smiled her way through most of the day and was juggling more than she could handle. By the end of the day, she had nothing left and part of her was resenting the fact that she'd get home and have to continue giving. Making dinner, cleaning, laundry, tidying up, even talking! So she'd push her husband away at the slightest sign that he might want or need anything.

As we dived deeper, it became clear that Karen hadn't learned how to get her own needs met. So it was time to learn. Eventually she shared with her husband what was happening and asked him to help her by giving her a hug when she walked through the door, handling dinner two nights a week, and running her a bath once a week. Essentially, the berating part was designed to save her resources so that she could keep going at work. And once she found an alternative solution, one that was actually better for her (and her husband!) this part could relax more because it knew she was being taken care of. Not surprisingly, these changes started to ripple out, and she made some important changes that led to more balance at work, too.

Love your parts. Find out what they're protecting you from. Negotiate a better way, and your life will change.

It's Never Too Late!

It really isn't. When life gets good, the difficult times are quickly forgotten. The TURN process that you're about to learn is going to teach you four specific, practical, and simple steps you can take to identify Primary Parts (plus less dominant parts, if you choose), learn how and why they operate the way they do, and ultimately understand and accept yourself more deeply. Following that, you'll begin to trust yourself in ways you haven't before, act on your intuition more, and naturally take steps forward. And for that, you'll have a structure for designing and taking strategic action.

Work is, for many of us, the place we choose to make a difference and give back for all we've received. Many of us feel incomplete when we're not doing this. So getting clear and moving forward is important. My strong suggestion for you at this time is to actively engage in the steps coming up in this book. Don't just *read* them—*do* them! I can promise you that, by going all in, you'll start to integrate the changes you feel, and that's the foundation of lasting change—which is what you want, right?

Chapter Four

The TURN Process

How do we identify and upgrade parts that aren't serving us anymore? How do we start to move with more ease toward what our heart wants? How do we get clear about what we really want and then get our scared, non-believing parts on board with the job of helping us?

TURN holds the essential ingredients. Time and again, I've witnessed the difference that these four steps make for people: From greater clarity of purpose to improved self-confidence; showing up more powerfully in difficult relationships; starting and growing a business; moving through career transition; getting back into the workplace after long periods of unemployment; and re-claiming their mojo! These tools continue to prove invaluable to those who practice them, and now I'm going to share them with you.

Here's how TURN breaks down:

Step One: TRANSFORM parts to support your vision

Step Two: UNWIND into clarity and ease

Step Three: RESOLVE to act on your intuition

Step Four: NEXT steps

Take a moment and write down a professional goal you have. Perhaps it's an element of something you're already moving toward that feels out of reach. Or something you've wanted for years. Or something else.

IMPORTANT NOTE: Please write something here that is specific and measurable, as opposed to a feeling. For example, *"I want to clarify what my next job is"* versus *"I want to feel happy."* Yes, feeling happy matters, but it's a step along the way. What I'd like you to write here is what you imagine will make you happy.

I want _____

Now, with that goal front and center, go ahead and walk through the four steps.

Step One:

Transform

Transform Parts to Support your Vision

Jean attended one of my TURN workshops. I remember at one point we were sitting on cushions on the floor, and she was talking about how she couldn't get her professional life moving again. As we talked, she shared a story about her husband, Jack.

Jean had been married for about forty-five years when Jack passed away. After he was gone, she was left feeling deeply alone and frightened. Jack had supported her in many ways: financially, yes, but perhaps the harder realization for Jean was the depth of his emotional, mental, and spiritual support. It was to such a degree that she was left not knowing how to get through life without him.

She could not figure out how to stand on her own two feet because she had been so reliant on him. She would stay at home all the time, was struggling to get back to work, and had isolated herself from family and friends.

As we quietly talked, I started to hear the conflict in Jean's voice. There were large parts of her that were clearly feeling bereft, apathetic, and stuck. But there was another part that was trying to be heard. That was the part that said, "We need to let go. We need to move and be closer to people who love us. We are okay, and we can do this." That part was hopeful, open, and nervously excited. As Jean talked and I guided her to greater awareness of these opposite parts inside her, two things started to happen simultaneously. She began to connect the dots of how much she had relied on her husband and isolated herself, and she started to open up to the idea of getting her life moving again.

Jean had been judging herself harshly for not being able to take steps forward, and, as we talked, she began to understand herself more deeply. She began to experience a freedom that she had not felt in a long time. Her face relaxed, her eyes glistened with relief, and she clapped her hands together in a moment of joy. A few months later, Jean moved back to her east coast life, where family and friends greeted her with open arms and she got back on the career track that gave her fulfillment. She was moving again.

Becoming aware of what stops us from having what we want starts with listening to the ways we speak to ourselves. We must pay attention to what the different parts of us are saying and then discover their underlying positive intention. Once we understand what is driving our Inner Critic, for example, we find that some of its old, unhelpful behaviors start to transform, and we begin to be kinder to ourselves and others. As a result of a shift like that, more of what we want comes into our lives. The job, the pay increase, the boss who treats us well, the company with a mission we love . . .

So let's start with the Inner Critic. It's a voice most of us are familiar with. It says things like, *"You can't do that," "You'll never win," "You'll never be good enough,"* and *"Look how you messed that up again; you're useless."* Our Inner Critic typically believes that We Will Never Measure Up. And so . . . we feel that we'll never measure up, and that feeling gets activated when things don't go the way we want. We don't get the job, and it reminds us that we don't measure up. We have a disagreement with a friend, and we feel it's because we don't measure up. We lose our husband and sink into the feeling of not measuring up.

More often than not, when our Inner Critic speaks up, people will typically do one of two things. Either

1) resist it and try to push it away, or 2) believe it and feel deflated. Neither reaction is effective. In order to transform this part that loves to use our worst fears against us, we must learn to hear, listen, and then get curious. If we saw a stranger on the street, and they were yelling about how terrible everyone and everything is, we might wonder with compassionate curiosity what had happened to them to cause them to act this way; or we might feel annoyed and walk quickly by; or we might pause and listen with curiosity. My point is that we probably would not take it personally, and that is how we need to be with our own harshest parts.

In the context of the Inner Critic, let's revisit this idea that every single part of us has positive intention. Our Inner Critic is no exception to this rule, but it has a way of showing up that probably made more sense when we were five than it does now that we're adults.

For example, a child who grows up with a highly critical parent will form that same voice/part inside of them. It's the child's way of keeping themselves in check internally, as the parent did externally. And it's a strategy to gain approval from the parent. To an adult, this level of internal, and often external, criticizing can be demoralizing, to say the least. It can lead to isolation, not feeling good enough, or even pushing people away by being overly critical (to self and/or others). All that said, the intention of the Inner Critic is positive—in this example, it's working hard to protect the inner child from getting hurt again by doing all (s)he can to gain the parent's love and approval.

As children we do whatever we must to make sure we belong and get our needs for love and approval met. We're completely and utterly dependent, which can be a difficult feeling to remember as adults. This is often the time when Inner Critics are born. If you reflect for a moment, does it feel like your Inner Critic has been with you for as long as you can remember? Well, it probably has, and now those old ways of coping need to be updated. So how do we do this?

I've already mentioned listening and getting curious, so let's start there. Have you ever wondered what your Inner Critic would say if it were given center stage? Well, you're about to find out!

Go ahead and allow your Inner Critic to speak out loud (or in your head if you're somewhere in public). That part of you has plenty to say, so let it talk. Remembering back to a time when you made a mistake is a great way to rouse the Inner Critic.

IMPORTANT NOTE: I'd like to mention here that each of our parts, whether we personally like them or not, are like most human beings. The roughest, meanest person can calm right down when their point of view is heard, acknowledged, and not judged. It's the same with all of your parts. When you listen and get curious about the motivations each part of you has, those parts of you that are vying for attention often start to calm down; because they're being acknowledged. So as you're writing what your Inner Critic is saying, do your best to receive the information from an objective "Oh, wow—that's genuinely interesting" perspective. This is just a part of your psyche; there is no true, imminent threat.

Go ahead now and take a couple of minutes to just listen to that part of you and jot down what you hear. You'll often find that by writing it down, you can deepen your understanding and sometimes be surprised.

YOUR TURN

Things my Inner Critic says:

(Think back on times you made a big mistake or took a huge risk. What was the inner dialogue?)

_____

_____

_____

The TURN Process: Step One

You've just taken one of the hardest steps. You've identified your Inner Critic as a part of you. What did you notice?

_____

_____

_____

_____

_____

_____

Now it's time for dialogue. In other words, now it's time to get into a two-way conversation with this part.

I'll take a moment to remind you that it is much more effective to do these exercises with pen and paper than loosely in your mind. If you want change, it takes doing things that are uncomfortable, and if this is uncomfortable for you, then there's probably some significant value that an unconscious part of you wants to avoid.

So here we go. Once again, identify your Inner Critic. Become aware of that part, and see if you can sense where it is in your body. How does it feel, and where do you feel it? Notice that for a minute. And don't worry too much if *feeling it* is challenging.

Now start to listen to what your Inner Critic is saying. It might even be criticizing this exercise or this book! If that part of you is not speaking yet, think of a professional risk you want to take (for example: leaving your job, asking for a pay raise, changing careers altogether) or a time when you messed up, broke something or failed catastrophically, and see if that gets it talking.

The next step is to start asking questions of your Inner Critic and really listening to the answers (instead of assuming you already know the answers and filling in the blanks yourself). If your Inner Critic is saying things like, *"You'll never be able to do that,"* a good question to ask might be, *"Why do you say that?"* Then pause, as if you'd just asked someone sitting next to you, and literally wait for an answer. Then, once you've heard the reply, you might ask, *"What is it you want for me?"* Then listen to that answer. Then ask, *"When did you come into my life? What was the event that brought you in?"* Or you could ask, *"What is your role in my life?"* There are no bad questions. The main idea here is to make sure you're addressing your Inner Critic as a separate part of you, and letting that part of you answer.

Go ahead now and ask one, two, or all of those questions, and just listen to the answers. You might be amazed. Write down what you hear. And as you do, notice what happens to your Inner Critic as you show curiosity and make a genuine effort to understand instead of resisting or arguing with it. If some of your own questions come to mind, feel free to ask those. You're in a conversation, and, honestly, anything goes; you might even find yourself getting sad or mad at this part of you. That's okay, too. Just keep the conversation open, and let that part of you respond. Trust me: You can *shout* it into submission for only a limited amount of time!

See you in a page or two. I've added some questions for you below. And, by the way: If you have another part that you'd prefer to dialogue with right now, please do go ahead.

IMPORTANT NOTE: If you complete this exercise only in your mind, you're unlikely to gain any real benefit or new information. If you do what's uncomfortable and identify where this part is inside you, and then stop and really listen to what it has to say, you might be surprised by what you hear. Thinking you already know what your Inner Critic or any part will say will simply cause you to experience very little that's new from these exercises. So watch for the part that might be saying something like, *"Eh, we don't need to do the exercise!"* or *"I already know what that part is going to say"* or even *"I don't have time to do this."* It's a trap!

YOUR TURN

Dialogue with your Inner Critic:

Why are you critical of me?

_____

_____

_____

_____

What is it you want for me?

_____

_____

_____

_____

When did you come into my life?

___

___

___

___

What is your role in my life?

___

___

___

___

What do you think about this career change I want to make?

___

___

___

___

What, if anything, would need to be in place for you to support me in making this change in my career?

_____

_____

_____

_____

Most people who perform this exercise notice that their Inner Critic begins to soften a little and also shares information that gives them a better (and unexpected) understanding of why it's being so harsh. Some people experience the softening as feeling a little more relaxed, less tense. Some find that they experience more compassion. And toward whom are you ultimately experiencing more compassion? *You.* When we're uncomfortable with a part, for whatever reason, it is common to attempt to disown it by ignoring it or shouting at it to stop. But when we disown a part of us, we send ourselves a message that something is wrong with us, and that shuts off some of our potential, some of our heart, and much of our clarity and courage. We are perfectly designed to handle the life we have lived, and appreciation for that can be liberating.

Now that you're clear on the Inner Critic, let's find an opposite part, a part that cheers you on and says things such as, *"You can do it!" "You're smart enough and deserving enough to have what you want." "You're ready!"* This might be your Supportive Inner Voice part. Then go ahead and repeat the previous steps. Start by identifying where that part is in your body and what it feels like. Then listen and/or write (thinking of a time you succeeded at something or were proud of yourself will bring this part out more easily), and then ask one or two questions and see what answers you receive.

Notice any difference in the quality of your voice when you talk with your Supportive Inner Voice, and notice any differences in how you feel during and afterward. Go ahead and give this part a name—you can even ask this part what it would like to be called. For some of you, it's been a long time since you connected with the feeling of believing in yourself, so if your Inner Critic keeps interrupting, politely ask it to wait.

YOUR TURN

Dialogue with your Supportive Inner Voice (I encourage you to give this part a name):

What talents do you think I have?

_____

_____

_____

_____

What is it you want for me?

_____

_____

_____

_____

When did you come into my life?

___

___

___

___

When did you last come out?

___

___

___

___

What is your role in my life? Or what role would you like?

___

___

___

___

What shall I call you?

_____

_____

_____

_____

What do you think about this career change I want to make?

_____

_____

_____

_____

What do you think about what the Inner Critic says about me?

_____

_____

_____

_____

If you were running the show, what would you have me do to move forward in my career?

_____

_____

_____

_____

✳ ✳ ✳

TRANSFORM is about listening deeply and learning from those parts of us that seem to put our best interests last and then discovering that the parts we like least are often the ones most dedicated to keeping us safe. The surprising result of this seemingly simple exercise is that people often experience an inner shift that empowers them and makes having what they want much easier because some of the resistance they've been experiencing transforms into ease.

Before you move on to **Step Two: UNWIND**, go ahead and write down three other parts you're noticing when it comes to your career changes, such as: the part that feels anxious, the part that hates my boss, the part that tries to find reasons to stay in bed. They might be playing a role in stopping you from moving forward in your professional life. Identify parts you struggle with. Don't worry about what you name them; you can ask them what they want to be called later. Schedule fifteen minutes to dialogue with one part each week.

Parts I'm noticing:

1. _____

2. _____

3. _____

It can be powerful to identify opposites, too, especially if you're not yet in touch with them.

EXAMPLES of opposites you might discover:

- A part that is a powerful negotiator, and an opposite part that's terrified of not being liked and therefore doesn't want to negotiate too powerfully.

- A part that's ready to go for that dream job you want, and a part that says, *"You're not good enough—so why bother?"*

- A part that wants to take more action and follow up with important contacts or opportunities, and a part that says, *"There's no point, you may as well go back to the couch."*

Do the dialogue exercise with them. Ask any additional questions that come to mind about the professional change you want to make. Trust your own curiosity, and listen to their answers.

YOUR TURN

List of three opposite parts to dialogue with:

PART	OPPOSITE PART
Powerful negotiator	*Afraid to ask for what I want*
1.	1.
2.	2.
3.	3.

Begin to listen and learn about the different parts of you that are playing a role in whether you do or don't have the career (or even life) you want. Be curious and kind rather than harsh and judging. We all have parts of ourselves that seem easy to reject and judge. Those are the parts most worthy of our love and understanding. In fact, appreciating the parts of yourself you find hardest to appreciate is the ultimate in freedom and self-acceptance; it's easier to make progress when shame, guilt, or fear isn't in the driver's seat or even running behind the scenes.

From this point on, assume that every part of you has a positive intention for you and that it's your job to discover what that intention is. As you accept and appreciate more of your selves, the better you will feel, and the more likely you are to go after the life you want.

Concluding this chapter and first step: **Transform parts to support your vision.** This tool can be used any time you find yourself being pulled in opposite directions. For example, you become aware of a part that strongly wants to quit your job and another part that is terrified of doing so. Or, the challenges can be even more subtle, such as a part that would like to look at job descriptions further afield versus a part that is convinced that's a waste of time and that you should stay closer to home. Use the dialogue tool of TRANSFORM any time you have a difficult decision to make, or you're trying to untangle internal conversations and move forward.

Now you've completed the first step, and you're ready to take the second step: UNWIND into clarity and ease. Before we head there, take a moment and jot down three new realizations you gained from TRANSFORM:

YOUR TURN

1. _____

2. _____

3. _____

   _____

   _____

   _____

Chapter Five

The TURN Process

Step Two:

Unwind

Unwind into Clarity and Ease

Did you know that brain activity changes when our brains have a chance to power down and rest? And when brain activity changes, the way we make decisions changes. The way you arrive at your professional goal is through a series of decisions, many of them important ones. Probably, like most people, you'd like to get to this next chapter of your professional life in the shortest amount of time. In order to do that, a rested brain is necessary; this will help you make your best, most time-saving decisions.

The value of unwinding is often underrated in this go-go-go world through which we speed. Idleness is judged. Success is confused with high stress, multi-tasking, and busyness. Our brains are so over-used that our capacity to make good decisions is greatly diminished. We over-use our minds, our intellects, and the more mental multi-tasking and decision-making we engage in (from what to say in an interview, to whether to invest money in getting our resume upgraded, to should you email an important contact), the more tired our brain becomes. And as our brain gets tired, it begins to behave differently. And so do we.

For those who do get to rest their brains at night, it's easier to face significant life decisions (changing career, changing your address, separating from a significant relationship) first thing in the morning because the brain has had time to shut off and rest. As the day wears on, it becomes easier to dive for the literal or metaphorical couch and quit the job search because stress and over-thinking lead to tiredness and lethargy. For this reason, naps and a meditation practice can prove invaluable. When we're tired, we're less aware of the long-term implications of our inaction. Why are we less aware? Because the parts of our brain that take into account all the complexities and implications of a decision we're making—from present possibilities to future scenarios and past experiences—shut down. And when they shut down, we're left with a decision to eat the donut because we can no longer connect with connect with the long term implications of eating that donut. Or we accept the salary we know isn't enough because we're exhausted from job hunting and have forgotten the consequences from the last time we did this.

What does this mean in the context of career change? It means that it's vital to make resting your mind as important as cleaning your teeth, walking your dog (or yourself), taking a shower, or eating lunch. TRANSFORM will help quiet your mind by giving it a voice. UNWIND is a step designed to get you out of your mind and into your body so that your brain can recharge.

YOUR TURN

A Three-Minute Exercise

Wherever you are as you read this book, I invite you now to allow a breath.

A deep, slow one.

And then another.

Take three deep, slow breaths all the way down into your belly. As you do so, allow yourself to notice what's around you; notice your belly as it fills with air and empties. Feel your feet on the floor, wiggle your toes, notice what you hear, smell any smells, and become aware of any sensations in your body—tingling, buzzing, tightening, opening, expanding, contracting, ease . . . If there are any conversations still happening in your mind, imagine yourself turning down the volume of those voices in your head until they're on mute and all you're aware of is what is around and inside you right here, right now.

And pause.

Breathe one more belly breath.

Pause again.

REPEAT 3x/DAY: When you wake, before lunch, and before sleep.

YOUR TURN

What do you notice when you slow everything down in this way and bring your attention into the present moment?

_____

_____

_____

_____

_____

_____

_____

_____

_____

When we're in the now, we open the doorway for something new to come in. Have you noticed how "a-ha!" moments, solutions to problems, and new realizations often come when you're relaxed—such as in the shower, right before falling asleep, and sometimes in the middle of the night or during a conversation. Usually, these moments will come when you're not focusing on them.

> *A client, Sarah, uncovered something extraordinary during our coaching. It wasn't a new thought, but it was profound in the sense that she rediscovered something that seemed to be so obvious. Sarah is a business owner; she helps large organizations tap into creativity in order to develop and generate greater collaboration and productivity. Prior to starting her business, she had done a lot of painting with watercolors but for some reason had gotten away from it, as happens to many of us. We get busy and forget about the things that most revive and energize us. As her business had grown, Sarah had forgotten about this artistic love of hers. As we coached, she remembered how revitalizing, energizing, and fun this had been for her, and she committed to ten minutes a day of painting, moving forward.*

She was really committing to ten minutes a day of brain rest.

Until this realization, Sarah was burning out in her business because her brain was being pushed to its limits with endless decisions regarding how to generate more income, how to attract new clients and handle existing ones—plus how to fit in daily life! There was no pause button, and stress was running her days and nights. Sarah knew that the way she was doing business needed to change, but she didn't have the mental capacity to redesign her strategy because she was simply too mentally tired.

Even though it seemed counter-intuitive to take a pause when there was clearly so much to do (SIDE NOTE: talk to the part that's convinced you don't have time for self-care activities or things you enjoy), *Sarah realized that the only way to expand her mental capacity and redesign how she was doing business was to give her brain a break.*

As Sarah added painting back into her life, she began to come up with ideas for enlarging her client base while working fewer hours. She found herself enjoying work more and started to clarify an inspiring, energizing vision for her business. Opportunities began to come her way. Sarah gave her brain a rest, and the results rippled out across her whole life. She had more energy and regained the deep feeling of satisfaction that had been there at the start of her business. And all because she rediscovered an activity that rejuvenated her deeply and then spent a mere ten minutes a day doing it.

In addition to the breathing exercise, I encourage you to choose an additional activity you enjoy that has perhaps taken a back seat or maybe something new you've been considering. Take a moment now and choose one way that would help you UNWIND. Even five minutes a day of meditation (there are many types, and this is especially powerful if you don't sleep well at night), painting, walking, cooking, dancing, or reading can really start to change things. What's one step you're willing to take to give your brain a break?

YOUR TURN

My one step to give my brain a rest is:

Time(s) of day I'll practice this step:

Amount of time I'll spend:

Endless mental chatter—parts that won't stop doing, doing, doing or feelings of brain fog and lethargy—closes the door to a place that exists inside every one of us. This place is where our deepest wisdom lives. It is the place that holds the solutions we're seeking and the place that knows how to get us what we most desire. If the door to this place is closed, we can find ourselves spiraling, repeating the same mistakes over and over, and living with a feeling that we are continually hitting a glass ceiling inside ourselves. Unwinding opens the door to this place of wisdom, and, as this door opens, our lives get easier and more enjoyable. They somehow seem to fit us better.

This place of wisdom is known by many names—intuition, gut, sixth sense, hunch, clairvoyance, ESP, discernment, foreknowledge, inspiration, perception, premonition, innate knowledge, second sight, and others. Having access to this place that I'll be referring to as "intuition" is like having access to your greatest superpower. And yes, every one of us has an intuitive wisdom that is communicating with us every day.

I invite you to put down this book, breathe, and take your one step every day for seven days. And during that UNWIND time, take a pause from your job search or career research and notice any benefits you receive. Do you find yourself feeling more ease? Are you more productive? Do you have more patience, sense of humor, or creativity?

YOUR TURN

Notes for one week later:
As a result of unwinding daily, I notice:

_____

_____

_____

_____

_____

Before we head to the third step, RESOLVE to act on your intuition, take a moment and jot down three new realizations you gained from UNWIND:

YOUR TURN

1. _____

2. _____

3.

Chapter Six

The TURN Process

Step Three:

Resolve

Resolve to Act on Your Intuition

Perhaps you're discovering your intuition for the first time, or maybe you're ready to act on it in areas of life where you hesitate, or you're simply ready to go to the next level and listen more deeply. Wherever you are on the journey is perfect, and there will *always* be further to go. Intuition isn't something you have or don't have access to. It could be a strong feeling or a subtle one. You might act on it when it comes to your best friends and ignore it when it comes to choosing an intimate partner. Overall, it's like a fine wine—it gets better, deeper, more complex, and way more fun over time.

- Jagdish Parikh is the author of several books, including *Intuition: The New Frontier of Management*. Parikh did a study at Harvard Business School with 13,000 executives from various cultures. The widely cited results showed that the respondents, both male and female, said that they used their left and right brain about equally but that they attributed 80 percent of their business success to acting on their intuition. In organizations, intuition has been credited with better hiring decisions, higher motivation among staff, and, in general, being able to suss people out more easily.

- August Kekulé discovered the molecular structure of benzene because of a daydream. He envisioned the classic Ouroboros symbol of a snake devouring its own tail, and that gave him the idea of the ring structure of the benzene molecule. This changed the way that scientists looked at problem solving by validating the use of intuitive intelligence as a part of the process.

- In 1961, a man named Ray Kroc was in his office trying to figure out whether to pay $2.7 million for a little string of eight restaurants called McDonald's. The story goes that he was in his office, and his attorney (and his Inner Critic) were saying, *"No! No, no, no, no, no, no, NO!"* while his body and his intuition were saying, *"Yes! You've got to do this. You've absolutely got to do this!"* He was literally throwing things across his office and shouting because he was so frustrated. His gut was saying one thing, and his head was saying another thing; he didn't know what to do. Well, of course, you know the decision he ultimately made. Ray Kroc went against the advice of his attorney, picked up the phone, and said, *"Buy it. Pay the $2.7 million."*

Reflect for a moment on various people who have come into your life—perhaps at a job interview, over coffee with a coworker, or maybe the first time you met your closest friend. Often, when we meet people, we get a feeling, a sense about them. We might find ourselves thinking, *"That person is wearing all the best clothes and saying all the right things, but something doesn't feel right."* Sometimes we trust that hunch and stay away, and other times our minds convince us that there's no obvious proof and we say "Yes" to something that ultimately backfires. And, of course, the opposite also happens. We meet someone and know instantly that they're a good person and someone we either want to work with or befriend.

Intuition is that "feeling," that "sense." It's our secret weapon, and the only way to access this wisdom is to slow down. That's why this third step comes after UNWIND. We cannot access our intuition through the clamoring of an Inner Critic and an overactive mind. When thoughts and conflicting parts are bombarding us, the doorway to our deepest truths remains closed. Intuition holds the accumulation of every experience we've ever had, the true desire of our heart, and the deep knowledge of what we're capable of, i.e., our potential. In short, our intuition has access to everything we've ever done well and done poorly, everything we've learned, experienced, seen, sensed, and heard, both directly and indirectly. And when we're faced with a decision, our intuition pours through all that information for the best possible choice and then communicates to us via one little signal that nudges us to do something: To speak our mind, follow up again after that interview, call our friend for help, take a break, say "No" to that job.

The more we act on these nudges, the more we learn what is and isn't our intuition, and the more we find ourselves living a life that increasingly feels like it belongs to us. Intuitive intelligence is our deepest, truest inner wisdom. It's guiding us all the time, and, when we allow ourselves to follow, it leads us to who we most want to be and what we most want.

The Good News!

The good news here is that intuition is a muscle. The more we use it and trust it, the stronger and clearer it gets. For some, the bad news is that we have to use it in order to strengthen it. You might feel a nudge and follow it only to discover that that wasn't your intuition after all! Making mistakes is part of getting good at anything in life. It might also mean following that nudge even when it's leading you to a frightening place. If you've been out of work for a while, it's very difficult to walk away from a job offer you know is wrong for you when faced with no other choices.

It's important to know that it's okay to take baby steps and take them one at a time. Baby steps means starting to act on little nudges so that, over time, your intuitive intelligence becomes something you learn to trust. For example, you could start by noticing what you feel when you wear different types of clothing and choosing the ones that feel good. You could pay attention to what sensations you feel in your body when you talk to different people and perhaps let yourself walk away if that's the nudge you're getting. You could stop holding back on something you've been wanting to say. Notice in different situations if you're drawn. Do you want to run away? Notice, when you're driving, if "something" tells you to take an exit but your GPS doesn't seem to agree—which do you follow? Notice if you rejected a thought about taking an umbrella with you because the sun was out—and later it rained. Intuition shows up in lots of small ways. Your intuition gives you a nudge, and it's unattached to whether you act on the nudge or not. That said, ignore it for too long, and nudges can become big shoves.

A woman named Kate recently attended my TURN workshop and shared a story from two years earlier. She and her husband were about to lose their home. They had two months before foreclosure, and Kate was out of work. Then she got a job offer, and what do you imagine her intuition said? It said, "Don't take the job." Now this woman had not been following her intuition. This was not a well-worked muscle for her, which meant that she did not trust what she was feeling, certainly not enough to follow it when so much was at stake.

I think we can all agree that this particular decision would be a hard call. Your intuition says, *"Don't take the job,"* but you've got two months before losing your home. Most would probably say, *"Okay, gut, nice knowing you. See you later. I'll pay the price."* Kate did just that. She accepted the job and saved their house.

Flash forward two years: Sitting in my workshop is a woman who feels unable to leave that same job that she does not enjoy at all, because she's now over-worked, very low on confidence, full of resentment, and doesn't trust that she'd make a better choice if she left. I asked her, "In hindsight, what would have happened if you'd turned that job down? If you'd said 'No'?" She told me that everything would have been okay. That house wasn't worth the loss of quality of life, nor the professional stagnation that Kate traded for it.

Hindsight is 20/20. Because of that, it can be a great place to reflect and learn. When we start trusting our intuition with the little things—*Turn left, not right; Call Mary, not Monica; Go here, not there*—we begin to start working the muscle with small, low-risk choices. Then, when we're faced with bigger, higher-risk choices—*Do I take this job I don't want or do I lose my home?*—we're better able to make a decision that is true for us, because we've seen those decisions work out enough times in the past. But that type of choosing is less likely to happen without a track record of comfort and confidence in your intuition.

Now it's time to explore your intuition.

YOUR TURN

My name for intuition is: _____

Recall a time that you felt your intuition and did *not* follow it. Write down what you felt, sensed, saw, and heard. Describe what happened and what helped you know it was intuition versus something else:

_____

_____

_____

_____

_____

_____

_____

_____

_____

_____

_____

_____

_____

_____

_____

Of the seven areas of life listed below, put a ✓ next to the areas where you tend to more willingly act on your intuition, and a **X** next to the areas where your trust is lower so you're more likely to put off taking action or to doubt yourself:

Physical   *Social*   *Career*   *Spirituality*
Intimate Relationship   *Family*   *Finances*

Dedicate a few minutes to exploring your relationship with your intuition by answering the following questions:

1. I believe my trust is lower in _____ area of my life because:

   _____

   _____

   _____

   _____

   _____

   _____

2. I believe my trust is higher in _____ area of my life because:

   _____

   _____

   _____

   _____

   _____

3. In order to trust my intuition more in _____ area of my life I need:

_____

_____

_____

_____

_____

_____

4. Some intuitive nudges I'm receiving regarding my career:

_____

_____

_____

_____

_____

_____

_____

5. Some ideas about which I'm unclear on whether the nudges I'm receiving are my intuition or something else:

_____

_____

_____

_____

_____

_____

6. Overall, what I'm noticing about how intuition is currently guiding my career decisions and action steps:

_____

_____

_____

_____

_____

_____

7. Two steps toward acting on my intuition more that I'm willing to take now are:

_____

_____

_____

_____

_____

_____

✽ ✽ ✽

Your intuition will show you the most efficient route to the job you want, the business model that's most sustainable, the people who you fit best with. I would not say that following your intuition is an *easy* way of living life. It certainly is not initially. But it's the most *authentic* one, and it will reap you the rewards that your heart and soul crave. While your mind is generally dedicated to keeping you in a life that is known and somewhat predictable, your intuition invites you to discover more of who you are and what you're capable of. It invites you into the unknown, to take risks, and it rewards you with fulfillment, confidence, and a sense of well-being.

Over the years, I can confidently say that almost everyone I've coached and trained wanted to expand their potential. If that's what you want, then trusting your intuition is the way. The journey is a daily, in-the-moment one. In terms of your career, it means choosing more steps that probably feel risky and scary, or even exciting. It means choosing the ones driven by, *"If I knew I'd be okay, I would . . . ."* and not choosing the ones driven by fear.

Go ahead and write down three intuitive steps you're now willing to take in the next one to three weeks with regard to your career. It might be a conversation, reaching out to someone in your network, applying for a job you really want, asking for help learning a new skill, or something else:

1. _____

_____

2. _____

_____

3. _____

   _____

BONUS EXERCISE: Start an Intuition Journal.

This is a great exercise to share with a friend.

For three months write down weekly ideas you sense might be intuitive. At the end of each week go through your list and journal some notes:

- Explore if the ideas you took action on were indeed coming from your wise intuition.
- Notice how you feel about the ones you didn't act on.
- What were the results of the ones you did?
- Become aware of what you sense is different about each idea, including where in your body each is generated. Do intuitive ideas feel different from others? In what ways?
- Jot down which ideas moved you closer to what you want, and which moved you further away.

Spend three months cultivating a relationship with your intuition. Allow yourself patience, and to take a little more risk each week. As with any relationship, when you give it attention it will morph, clarify and by the end of three months you'll experience a deeper understanding of and trust in the decisions you make.

※ ※ ※

You've successfully completed the first three steps of the TURN process. These were all inner-game steps. Feel free to go back to any or all of them at any time. I've made this process linear for ease, but these are all tools in your belt now, to be used in the ways that work best for you.

By this point in the book, I hope that you're feeling some readiness to get into action, that you understand some of your internal drivers a bit better, and that you are feeling greater ease and perhaps inspiration. But before we head into action and strategy with the fourth and final step—NEXT Steps—take a moment and jot down three new realizations you gained from RESOLVE:

YOUR TURN

1. _____

2. _____

3. _____

Chapter Seven

The TURN Process

Step Four:

Next

Next Steps

This final step of the TURN process is about creating a plan that you are energized to follow. For this to happen, it's helpful to have two things in place: 1) A Clear Goal and 2) An Effective Strategy.

If you're going to apply for a job that you don't really want or are flitting back and forth between different job titles, unsure of where to focus, you will be slowed down in your search. If you are spending six hours a day job hunting and find that that demoralizes you, or you're trying to handle networking events like an extrovert—when you're an introvert—you will be slowed down.

Before I continue, let's look at what can happen when we finally decide we are ready to take some important steps. Fear can come up. And if that's happening for you right now, just know that you're having a very normal response. You might not even recognize it as fear if you're used to defining "fear" in terms of a racing heart or nervousness. It might show up as procrastination or apathy. It can be tricky. So . . . if you're ready to get into action, feel free to jump ahead to the "1) A Clear Goal" section on page 108. If you're hesitant—read on.

Fear

It's important to note that, when we start to take steps toward a new job we want, or become ready to ask our boss if we can work from home one day a week, or take the leap into a new profession, it's common to feel conflicted about the impending change. This can be exacerbated externally by reacting to other people's opinions, and internally by our own Inner Critic, Supportive Inner Voice, Fearful Child, and other parts.

As you begin to imagine calling that important contact, handing in your resignation, telling your spouse you want a change, or even simply sitting down to do some research, you might find that fearful, resistant parts start to chime in. Perhaps you start thinking:

"This isn't that important—I'll get to it later." "I'll just be disappointed if I do this." "Am I doing this right? Probably not." "Ohhhh, that's a bad idea. It'll never work out." "What am I thinking? I could never afford to make a change like this." "I'm too busy for this."

This is fear talking, and it's very normal. In fact, if you're *not* feeling fear and/or resistance about the unknown, you're probably not moving in the right direction.

Fear loves to remind us of all the ways we might fail, and it can be extremely convincing. Fear might run stories of ultimate doom, death, and devastation all in service of keeping us safe and away from change. Or it might show up in more subtle, seemingly rational ways, such as convincing us that cleaning the house and talking to our friend for an hour are *really* a much higher priority than applying for that job.

The result of fear can be confusion or even wasting time by doing a lot of stuff that is (albeit unconsciously) designed by our fearful, protective parts to keep us exactly where we are: Comfortable, safe, and nowhere closer to what we want. If you're noticing that this is happening to you right now (if you're not making progress, it probably is), go back to TRANSFORM, and work with the part(s) of you who are afraid, numb, or pretending not to care, until you're ready to take a step.

RESOURCE: Go to www.ClarityUnlimited.com and watch my TEDx talk about Facing Fear.

Now, with the assumption that you're possibly a bit nervous but ultimately ready to get clear and design an action plan, let's get going.

---

1) A Clear Goal

If you see yourself in one or more of these scenarios, you're not clear:

- Applying for the same kind of job you've always applied for, knowing there's something more
- Wishing you knew how to combine two or three job ideas you have

- Searching for job titles and not feeling like you fit anywhere
- Daydreaming about starting your own business while you apply for jobs
- Daydreaming about closing your business
- Not wanting to do *anything*—you just want to run away!
- Enjoying what you're doing but knowing this isn't it
- Not knowing what you want

When you're clear, you know what job you're looking for. You know what it's called (maybe it has more than one name) or, at least, what the required skills are. You might wonder if you can really have it or if it even exists, but, ultimately, you're clear about what you want. There's a difference between being unclear, and doubting whether you deserve what you want or doubting that you have what it takes to get it.

When you're unclear, it shows up everywhere: In your conversations (you might notice puzzled looks on people's faces), in your cover letters and resume, and in your search. Employers want employees who are excited about the job and who know it's what they want. The people you meet are being bombarded by requests for help, so it's vital that you can communicate clearly, succinctly, and memorably what you're looking for. With the level of competition in today's market, you can't afford not to be clear about what you want.

Most people focus on their skills when it comes to looking for a job or starting a business. They ask, *"What do I do well?"* and search for job descriptions that they can fulfill. But your skills are only about one quarter of the picture. A clear goal consists of clarity about four elements:

1. Your skills
2. Organization—the type of organization you want to work for
3. People—the kind of people you want to work with and for
4. Benefits—salary/income, retirement, commuting distance, environment, professional training, travel requirements, and more

To help you clarify these four areas, I designed a tool called the Clarity Matrix. It's a process that helps people get a clear picture of what they want (there's a

Job Matrix and a Business Owner Matrix). Once you are clear about all four areas, you have a complete picture of what you want. This will laser-focus your job search and give you insights into what matters most to you. The Clarity Matrix also drives your interview questions by clearly showing you your deal breakers and points of negotiation.

Consider for a moment the potential downsides of looking only for a job you can do. By ignoring the organization's values or the temperament of the people, you could end up in a toxic environment. And over time, that can only harm your confidence levels, skill proficiency, and enjoyment of life. It might be a slow burn, but it will burn.

Your first step in NEXT is to make sure you're as clear as you can be. Here's a resource for you:

RESOURCE: Go to www.ClarityUnlimited.com and download the Clarity Matrix that fits you best.

IMPORTANT NOTE: I do want to mention that clarity is sometimes related to readiness. For some, it takes time to prepare for the changes they intuitively or consciously know will be needed once they get clear.

Kim was looking for a marketing/writing job in Silicon Valley, California. Unfortunately, Kim didn't want to work in Silicon Valley. She didn't like almost anything about the culture and business environment. She thought about moving across the country but brushed that idea aside—for almost two years. And then, after one-too-many rejection letters (or, even worse, no response at all) and the lack of organizations that aligned with her values, she looked outside of California. Kim was finally ready to move and deal with a significant life change if she found a job. It took about two months. She was flown in for an interview and hired. She knew it was the right place, and they knew she was the right fit. Once she was ready, it happened quickly.

Be gentle with yourself if you sense that you have some parts who need time to get ready for a change. Dialogue with them. Take a baby step every day so that you know you're moving forward and not stagnating.

If you know you're unclear, this is a good time to pause and complete your Clarity Matrix.

2) An Effective Strategy

According to Pareto's Principle, 80 percent of the results we get in life come from 20 percent of the actions we take—which means that only a small percentage of what we're doing actually helps us move toward our goal. Which really is great news. I hope you're feeling relief in the knowledge that there's probably a ton of stuff you're spending time and energy on that you no longer have to!

But how does this happen? How do so many people end up doing so many things that are—bottom line—not helpful? It happens because we get carried away by our mind, rather than checking in with our wise, intuitive self, who has more discernment. We work on autopilot a lot of the time, instead of pausing and considering whether what we're about to do is necessary or helpful in the context of the bigger picture, our goal.

With this in mind, we're going to move into planning. I strongly encourage you to take yourself off autopilot—both when you're planning and certainly once you start to follow your plan. Check in as you go. Ask: *Is that the best next step? Does that step make sense to my gut and my brain?* If you get a "Yes" from both, keep going. If you get a "No," pause. If you get a "Maybe," find out which part is a "Yes" and which part is a "No," and then adjust accordingly. Essentially, I'm suggesting that you plan with awareness.

Your Strategic Plan

Here we go. By this point, you are, I hope, clear (you can include getting clarity about what you want in this plan), off autopilot, and ready to write up a plan for your career search.

I do want to be very clear that what I'm outlining in the next few pages is a generic—but effective—approach. It's designed to be changed, built on, and certainly customized. It's a starting place. You might need something different or more specialized, and if you need help figuring that out, you know where we are. ☺

The three core elements of an effective career-transition strategy are outlined here. For now, just read, and if something additional jumps into your mind, jot it down:

1. Resources

It's important to identify what resources you need to succeed:

   a. **Finding/Identifying Jobs:** Craigslist, Glassdoor, Indeed, Monster and other online job forums, job boards, your target organization's website, in-person networking/professional groups, plus more general research that reveals your passions and values.

b. **Building Skills:** Staying current with industry knowledge, relevant skill-building training such as resume writing, negotiating, interviewing, networking, business-model design, communication styles, personal branding, using social media, clarifying what you want.

c. **Personal Strengths:** Personality tests such as Strengths Finder, Enneagram, Disc, and Kolbe Index can be useful ways to gain a better understanding of yourself and the environments where you fit best.

2. People

Clarify who you need to help you get where you want to go. Playing lone wolf will slow you down and demotivate you over time:

a. **An accountability buddy**, group, or online forum you know you can count on for career-transition support.

b. **A coach** to help you get clear about what you want, help you face and move through your fears, and then get you strategically to your goal.

c. **Recruiters** to search for you, the names of **hiring managers**, contacts in **organizations** that you're interested in.

d. **Testimonials** from people who will happily vouch for your professional credibility and skills.

e. **Emotional support:** Who can you talk to? Exercise with? Where do you go for support on the difficult days?

3. Strategic Plan

Simply put, your strategic plan is how you organize your priorities into the time you have. When you're in career transition, I suggest that rather than a goal date for landing that job, you have a check-in date instead. Set a clear intention to get the career or job that you want, and then spend every day going for it. Set a check-in date for three months out. That date is designed for you to review what you're doing, evaluate your progress, and make adjustments.

Measure your accomplishments as you go, and treat the journey as if it's a marathon. Sometimes a goal date simply adds stress and can exacerbate a sense of failure should you arrive at that date without a job. Make a plan, detach yourself from the timeline, schedule check-ins, and go for it.

Remember that unexpected things happen in life, and you'll adjust as you go along. It's very important to choose activities that you know you'll do. If you really hate networking meetings and know yourself well enough to know that you just won't go, find another way to meet people (for example: one-on-one lunches or Skype/Google Hangout calls), or find another way to re-frame networking in your mind.

NETWORKING EXAMPLE: If you're an introvert, then maybe huge group meetings might not be the way to go—or if you do go (to hear a relevant speaker, for example), be strategic ahead of time. Find out who's going and choose a couple of people to approach and meet. Find out a little about them so you have something to talk about. Decide ahead of time how long you'll stay, and give yourself permission to leave if you're having a difficult time. Even deciding what you'll say when you're ready to leave can be helpful. Ideally, take a friend, but the main thing is to have some sort of plan in mind before you go.

Now that you understand the three core elements—Resources, People and Strategic Plan—it's time to create your plan. Use the pages in this book, your computer, or some paper and a pen.

I've provided an outline below. Go ahead and fill in the blanks for Resources and People, and then you'll pull it all together into a first draft of your Strategic Plan.

Start by writing your professional goal here, and, as always, make it specific and measurable.

My professional goal is:

_____

_____

Go ahead and complete the following lists for Resources and People based on the goal that you've stated above. Then you'll use this information in your strategic plan.

1. Resources

- List four places where you can consistently research types of organizations you might want to work for. It's less relevant whether they have job openings and more important that you find places that match your values. Feel free to search internationally (Google key words; magazines—*Fortune, SHRM;* local, national, and international papers):

i. _____

ii. _____

iii. _____

iv. _____

- Capture a list of four places you'll consistently use to find open jobs (include both on- and off-line) (Monster, Indeed.com, job boards):

    i. _____

    ii. _____

    iii. _____

    iv. _____

- If helpful, list a free or paid training or personality test that might assist you:

    _____

- List skills you know you need assistance with (such as clear goal, resume writing, updating LinkedIn Profile, approaching hiring managers, developing relationships with your network, building confidence, job-seeking strategy, unwinding!):

    i. _____

    ii. _____

    iii. _____

    iv. _____

    v. _____

- List one or more networking groups you can attend:

    i. _____

    ii. _____

    iii. _____

- Other resources that would be useful:

    i. _____

    ii. _____

iii. _____

iv. _____

2. People

- List five organizations you're especially interested in ("target orgs"):

    i. _____

    ii. _____

    iii. _____

    iv. _____

    v. _____

- List five hiring managers of jobs you're interested in:

    i. _____

    ii. _____

    iii. _____

    iv. _____

    v. _____

- List people you know directly or indirectly who are working at or have worked at the organizations you're interested in:

  i. _____

  ii. _____

  iii. _____

  iv. _____

  v. _____

- List five people who you can talk to or have an informational interview with for industry- or job-specific information:

  i. _____

  ii. _____

  iii. _____

  iv. _____

  v. _____

- List four people or organizations to reach out to for strategic support (such as clear goal, resume/cover letter writing, updating social media, relationship building, communication):

i. _____

ii. _____

iii. _____

iv. _____

- List up to three people who would be motivational support (to talk to about your challenges, glean advice from, cheer you up, celebrate with you):

  i. _____

  ii. _____

  iii. _____

- List up to three people who could be part of a weekly/monthly/quarterly brainstorming or mastermind group:

  i. _____

  ii. _____

  iii. _____

- Who might be a powerful mentor for periodic advice?

  _____

- Other people you'd like on your team:

  i. _____

  ii. _____

  iii. _____

  iv. _____

  v. _____

3) Strategic Plan

The following is an outline that many of my out-of-work clients have used successfully. Be sure to make it your own, based on your energy ups and downs, family commitments, work hours, or other unchangeable scheduling issues (you might be working). The idea is to try something organized and then adjust as needed. As I mentioned earlier, sometimes focusing for shorter periods of time leads to greater productivity. Set an end time. You can always run over. Read through the following schedule, and edit it to fit you and your lifestyle. By the time you complete it, you should have a strategic-plan outline for the next week or so. Resources and People will probably be updated as you go from week to week.

WEEKLY SCHEDULE

Monday 9–11 am: Research #1: New jobs, possible careers, right-fit job titles, and organizations you're interested in (to work there or just as a model of what you'd like).

Monday 1–3 pm: Respond #1: Apply to jobs, reply to interview requests, emails, thank-you letters, follow-ups, or any other immediate actions.

Monday 5–6 pm: MASTERMIND/Brainstorming group call, 15 minutes per person.

✳ ✳ ✳

Tuesday 9–11 am: Outreach #1: Connect with people who can refer you, brainstorm with you, contacts you're building a relationship with.

Tuesday LUNCHTIME: Relationship-building meeting.

Tuesday 2–3 pm: Learning #1: Schedule a coaching call, time to update your resume, learn a new software program or other skill.

✳ ✳ ✳

Wednesday 9–11 am: Research #2: New jobs, possible careers, right-fit job titles, and organizations you're interested in (to work there or just as a model of what you'd like).

Wednesday 1–3 pm: Respond #2: Apply to jobs, reply to interview requests, emails, thank-you letters, follow-ups, or any other immediate actions.

✳ ✳ ✳

Thursday 9–11 am: Outreach #2: Connect with people who can refer you, brainstorm with you, contacts you're building a relationship with.

Thursday LUNCHTIME: Relationship-building meeting.

Thursday 2–3 pm: Learning #2: Schedule a coaching call, time to update your resume, learn a new software program or other skill.

✳ ✳ ✳

Friday 9–12 noon: Administrative: Update resume, update social media, non-urgent email, research networking groups to attend, reach out to schedule support for the skills you listed earlier.

Friday 3 pm onward: Something *fun* to celebrate your productive week.

Your final step is to enter this schedule into a calendar that you use—on paper or online. Choose a start date, and begin.

And that's it. You just completed NEXT.

You now have tools to deal with your inner game: TRANSFORM, UNWIND and RESOLVE. Plus, you have the three core elements of an effective career-transition strategy, and a first-draft strategic plan to follow: NEXT.

Congratulations, you have successfully completed the four steps of TURN!

TURN is a powerful process which, when practiced, can help you move more smoothly and effectively through your career transition. One reason it works is because this process addresses the inner game as well as the outer game, the emotional and mental sides of change—both are necessary to get what we want. Many people will get into action without getting their protective Primary Parts on board, and that leaves them spinning their wheels. Others will do the work of getting their Primary Parts on board but then not take action. To get where our hearts most want us to go, we must be congruently aligned with our best selves and off the couch.

Through the work we do, we all have an opportunity to make a positive impact with our lives, a splash that leaves other people and places better than we found them. This rewards us with a sense of meaning and fulfillment. But to have this, we must be willing to break away from conditioning and beliefs that seduce us into remaining the same. That frighten us away from the change we most crave. We must be willing to walk away from unsupportive relationships and to invite in a more like-minded tribe. We must, ultimately, be willing to find out if we can, if we actually care enough, if we have what it takes, if we do deserve our dreams, and if we are as powerful, brilliant, and impactful as we sense. We must be willing to trust our deepest wisdom. We don't have to take *huge* risks. We can take risks that feel more manageable. But we must be willing to do *something*. Small. Large. It doesn't matter. But do *something*.

There isn't a leader in the history of the world who didn't embrace these edges. Gandhi, Mother Teresa, Martin Luther King, Oprah Winfrey, Barack Obama, Eleanor Roosevelt, the list continues.

I'll close with a story of courageously following intuition, and I hope this final story inspires you to trust your deepest wisdom and do *your* next *something*.

Chapter Eight:

Rwanda

There's a country in East Africa that is better known for the atrocities of war it has suffered than for the striking beauty of its endless rolling hills and unusually high number of women in government positions. Rwanda sits nestled amidst a chain of east African countries: the Congo, Uganda, Tanzania, and Burundi. It is known as the Land of a Thousand Hills. In 1994, approximately 800,000 people were wiped out by genocide.

That history had always struck me, lingering in ways I couldn't quite comprehend. I found myself reading autobiographies of genocide survivors, and I grew curious about how a country recovers from something so devastating. Not just in terms of the loss of human life but also in the rebuilding of trust, relationships, industry, and economy. I'd sit in my Honolulu hillside home reading and pondering, part of me wincing at the graphic stories of suffering and part of me inspired by the country's ability to recover from such devastation. But even with this clear interest, I was still floored when, one day, the wise, intuitive voice inside me whispered, *"It's time to go. It's time to go to Rwanda."*

By this point, I was fairly familiar with this intuitive part of me in the area of my professional life, so I trusted its call. But there were still parts that felt afraid. Part of me was immediately worried about physical safety, another part about money. *What about the projects I was currently working on and the organization I supported, not to mention being away from home— and would my home be okay?* Many questions, from a plethora of internal players, began to bombard me:

"Why?" "For how long?" "What are you going to do there?" "What about your apartment?" "How much money will you need?" "Where will you stay?" "What will you wear?!" "Is it safe?!"

I knew people in many countries around the world. But Rwanda was a blank slate, a new beginning waiting to happen. I knew that accepting this intuitive invitation was right, and I knew it meant taking a big risk and walking away from everything that was familiar. Part of me sensed that I was being called to do something

BIG. Those were the words in my head, *"This is going to be BIG."*

That was my inspiration: BIG. Wow, I lacked clarity! I couldn't even put into words what I was good at professionally at that time. Over the years, I'd started small side businesses offering services that ranged from administrative assistance, to office organization, to space planning. I'd stumbled into a multitude of diverse professions, including life insurance sales, secretary, nanny, barista, interior designer, magazine editor, writer, telesales, and, more recently, project and people management. And now I was being called to do this BIG thing in a faraway land, with absolutely no clue how to talk to people and ask for help, because, at that time, I didn't know what the heck to say about what I had to offer.

But, apparently, that was okay.

The months it took to prepare for my departure went surprisingly smoothly. Have you noticed that when we take risks that honor who we deeply are, we tend to be supported? Some say such things as, *"The Universe conspires to help us,"* and I like that idea. Think of a time you made a clear decision. Did you notice that things seemed to fall into place? Well, that's what this was like.

At the very beginning, when I first sat with the idea of leaving for an indefinite time, there were so many conflicting voices competing for attention inside me that I couldn't see how it was possible. Parts of me kept throwing up images of all the things that could go wrong if I jumped out of my job and my life in such a way. But, slowly, I took actions that helped the fearful parts of me feel safer and, subsequently, more open to the idea of going. I kept remembering that I probably would not have been given the intuitive whisper if my entire life would fall apart as a result. With each step, more and more parts of me got on board and started to trust in this change.

For the part of me afraid of being so far from home, I signed up for Skype so I could speak with friends and family. For the part worried about having enough money, I saved enough to keep me going for a few months. For the physical fear I was feeling, I read up about the current political climate. For the part that needed some sort of time frame, I narrowed the trip down to three months. And for the part that loves adventure, I booked a flight into Cairo, Egypt, in January and out of Johannesburg, South Africa, in March. Then I did one more thing, for the part that needed to know someone in this completely unknown place: I found one contact over there, my now-dear-friend Mila, who was heading up Generation Rwanda. She agreed that I could volunteer for a couple of hours a week, interviewing orphans of the genocide about their experience during and since, which calmed the part of me that was worried about having too much time and nothing to do. An amazing start, for sure. Not BIG, not yet. But a great start. I felt humbled and grateful.

It took me approximately eight months to arrive in Rwanda after that initial, *"It's time to go to Rwanda"* message. There was pre-departure preparation time, which included a large number of vaccines and visas. Then, once I landed in Cairo, I chose to spend a couple of weeks travelling via land to Rwanda. I started by taking a noisy train through Egypt, and then a huge, gray, military-looking ship across to Sudan, a broken-down desert bus through the Nubian Desert at night to the capital city of Khartoum, followed by a small, dusty van ride with broken seats across the fields of Ethiopia. I jumped on a plane for the final leg, and Mila and I met up in Kigali (Rwanda's capital) that same day. The interviews began a few days later.

The survivors of the genocide were now teenagers, and they had experienced atrocities that most of us would find difficult to comprehend. I was interviewing these young adults so that the organization I represented, Generation Rwanda, could share their stories with potential donors, thereby giving these young adults an opportunity to go to university. Every single one stated with passion and a level of wisdom that seems to be granted to those who've experienced deep suffering that they wanted to give back to their country and ensure that such an atrocity never happened again. It was an honor and a privilege for me to get to know them.

Was it BIG? Yes. It was. Was it the kind of BIG I believed I was there for? No, it wasn't. About three weeks in, a very impatient part of me began playing with the idea of finding something else—maybe even leaving Rwanda. That part felt frantic to find this BIG thing, and all the waiting was driving her nuts! After all, I'd upturned my entire life and travelled halfway around the world. If it was meant to be BIG, I wanted BIG, and I wanted it NOW!

I told people what I wanted, in this very vague way. Quite frankly, they thought I was out of my mind. *"You don't arrive in Rwanda and expect to get a paid position after three weeks! It takes months of application processes from outside the country, if you're even lucky that way!"* The naysayers abounded and definitely triggered parts of me that were wondering what the heck I was doing, but I had a stronger connection to the part who knew intuitively that something was on its way. I just didn't know when, where, or what. So even though part of me was pushing to leave the volunteer position, my wise intuition clearly said, *"Do not quit."* So I once again followed that, albeit impatiently.

Then one day the interview location was changed to a new house, a big white mansion with pillars at the front steps and a long, steep, black tarmac driveway winding up to it. It was a hot day, and I panted my way up the driveway to conduct a set of interviews with two brothers who had hidden in a tree for the 100 days of the genocide. They'd survived by climbing down and stealing food in the middle of the night from a nearby orphanage. As I arrived at the door, I was met by Alissa. She was warm and welcoming, and I felt at ease with her right away. Once the interviews were complete, it was an obvious "Yes" to stay and chat for a while. I shared with her about my background and this BIG thing I believed I was in Rwanda to do.

Somehow she managed to ask questions that elicited clear answers from me about my professional background. I found myself communicating clearly. She listened closely and then, with quiet certainty, said, *"You've got to talk to my husband, Josh."*

Josh Ruxin is the founder and director of the Access Project in Rwanda, an initiative of the Center for Global Health and Economic Development at Columbia University. He was also, at that time, the country director of the Millennium Village Project. He led a team of people who were working tirelessly to end extreme poverty in a particularly hard-hit area of the country.

The model used by the Millennium Village Project (MVP) essentially teaches sustainable agriculture, health, education, and micro-finance practices as well as implements needed infrastructure changes for communities living in deep poverty. In Rwanda, the project served a population of approximately 50,000. Bottom line... MVP was working hand-in-hand with communities to cultivate self-supporting villagers and villages. Now that was BIG. Part of me was excited, and then I became very aware of another part that was suddenly very frightened.

I interviewed with Josh about a week later, and he invited me to spend a week out at the project site and then come back with an evaluation of what I saw was needed. For one week, I lived in a concrete room with a trash-bin-sized blue plastic bucket in the corner filled with cold water for bathing. I walked every day along a dusty road to a sparse concrete building and asked difficult questions of people from a completely different culture, attempting to elicit honesty and often not knowing what to do when I knew it would take longer than a week to earn that level of trust. And at the end of each day, I crawled under a mosquito net, wrapped myself in a stiff single sheet, and literally passed out from mild panic and growing exhaustion from being so completely out of my element in rural Rwanda. I returned to Kigali a week later—exhausted, exhilarated, and with a spreadsheet as long as my arm. It listed all the challenges that I saw and potential solutions.

When I showed Josh the spreadsheet, he said, *"You know, I had a sense a lot of this was going on. You're hired."*

What?! Surely this was meant to be harder?! I worked out there as a management consultant (had to change that return flight). I completed the project's first strategic plan and was part of a small, brilliant team. We updated and added much-needed policies and procedures in the office, organized the first formal employee evaluation, and implemented some essential new-hire and organizational adjustments. The wrong people left, the right people came, and things were much more efficient and effective.

It was exciting. It wasn't BIG. It was HUGE. And months later, when my contract ended, I came home a little disoriented.

It wasn't easy being out there (that's a massive understatement). I'm still not sure where I found strength on the really hard days when going shopping or eating my favorite Thai meal or curling up in my own bed as ways of coping just weren't options. I chose to stay when most of me wanted to flee. An intuitive nudge—*"It's time to go to Rwanda"*—changed my entire life. Not because I recognized the nudge, but because I acted on it. I trusted it. And I learned to trust myself in a deeper way as a result. Africa had been tugging at my heart since I was sixteen years old, and Rwanda was my first visit. That experience turned out to be an important part of my purpose because of who I became as a result of trusting my wise intuition over my fear and discovering parts of myself that I would not have discovered had I stayed home. The people I met, the skills I developed, what I learned about community and relationships and patience . . . Saying "Yes" to the pull of Africa led me to access more of my potential than I could have ever imagined, and my reward for taking that leap was a level of fulfillment I'd craved for as long as I could remember.

That's been the ongoing gift of sensing, trusting, and acting on my intuition. In exchange for getting congruent with parts that are truly, authentically me, I've gained an ever-deepening feeling of fulfillment, peace, and belonging—plus a career that continues to expand, challenge, and fit me.

Maybe you're aware of something that your intuition is nudging you to do, and maybe you're wondering what to do about it. Maybe this nudge has been going on for a long time, or maybe it's recent. It takes courage to say, *"Yes, I'll listen, and I'll act on this."* And you don't have to do it alone. Nor do you have to do it in one enormous leap. But do remember . . .

Your "Africa" is out there waiting for you to say, "Yes." It might not be BIG; it might be something quite small and powerful, like a conversation that will forever change the quality of your life. Don't judge. It's uniquely yours, whatever it is and wherever it's guiding you. Those intuitive nudges are trying to lead you home to the life that you're seeking. But it takes courage to take steps in the direction of who you know yourself to be.

Want to experience and express your full potential? This is how. Want to feel joy, peace and fulfillment? You get that by being willing to be and live as the real You. Want to know your best-fit career? Deepen your awareness of the parts that want to stop you from changing, dialogue with them, and then act on the intuitive pulls and sudden inspired ideas that surface.

As Nelson Mandela so wisely stated: "It always seems impossible until it's done."

I encourage you to keep going. Until it's done.

About the Author

Clara Chorley helps professional women and men around the world gain clarity about what's next in their careers and then take strategic steps to get there—whether that means up-leveling their current career or figuring out something new.

She is the CEO and founder of Clarity Unlimited and has an extensive and unique international background as a career coach and consultant, professional speaker, humanitarian, and insatiable explorer.

She grew up in England and has lived in Germany, India, the Hawaiian Islands, Rwanda, and Northern California, USA. She has traveled and worked across five continents and forty-four countries with organizations as diverse as Fortune 500 Ernst and Young, to the humanitarian Millennium Village Project.

In addition to being a successful and happy entrepreneur, Clara has been a volunteer for international humanitarian causes for more than fifteen years. She is author of the book *TURN: 4 Steps to Clarity in your Career*. Clara has been interviewed by multiple radio and television shows, including San Francisco's "View from the Bay," and was featured in the documentary film *Achieve Your Ultimate Success*. She is an international speaker and proud TEDx presenter. Clara is trained in Voice Dialogue, a certified facilitator and organizational diagnosis consultant.

Resources

Struggling to get clear about the job you want?

Interested in scheduling a complimentary Discovery Call to see how we might support you?

Looking for a speaker for your next event?

www.ClarityUnlimited.com

www.ingramcontent.com/pod-product-compliance
Lightning Source LLC
Chambersburg PA
CBHW070620300426
44113CB00010B/1596